4/81

Books by W. S. Merwin

POEMS

The Compass Flower   1977
The First Four Books of Poems   1975
(INCLUDING THE COMPLETE TEXTS OF
*A Mask for Janus, The Dancing Bears,
Green with Beasts* AND *The Drunk in the Furnace*)
Writings to an Unfinished Accompaniment   1973
The Carrier of Ladders   1970
The Lice   1967
The Moving Target   1963
The Drunk in the Furnace   1960
Green With Beasts   1956
The Dancing Bears   1954
A Mask for Janus   1952

PROSE

Houses and Travellers   1977
The Miner's Pale Children   1970

TRANSLATIONS

Selected Translations 1968–1978   1979
Osip Mandelstam, Selected Poems (WITH CLARENCE BROWN)   1974
Asian Figures   1973
Transparence of the World (Poems by Jean Follain)   1969
Voices (Poems by Antonio Porchia)   1969
*Products of the Perfected Civilization
(Selected Writings of Chamfort)*   1969
*Twenty Love Poems and a Song of Despair
(Poems by Pablo Neruda)*   1969
Selected Translations 1948–1968   1968
The Song of Roland   1963
Lazarillo de Tormes   1962
The Satires of Persius   1960
Spanish Ballads   1960
The Poem of the Cid   1959

WRITINGS TO AN UNFINISHED ACCOMPANIMENT

W. S. MERWIN

WRITINGS TO AN UNFINISHED ACCOMPANIMENT

New York ATHENEUM 1980

Some of the poems have appeared in the following periodicals:

EARLY ONE SUMMER: *Choice*
EYES OF SUMMER: *Quarterly Review of Literature*
END OF SUMMER: *Hudson Review*
THE DISTANCES: *Hudson Review*
LOOKING BACK: *Poetry*
SONG OF MAN CHIPPING ARROWHEAD: *Poetry*
THE SILENCE BEFORE HARVEST: *Kayak*
CAT GHOSTS: *Chelsea*
LETTER TO THE HEART: *The Nation*
MEMORY OF THE LOSS OF WINGS: *Poetry*
THE OLD BOAST: *Kayak*
THE DAY: *Poetry*
THE CLEAR SKIES: *Hudson Review*
TO BE SUNG WHILE STILL LOOKING: *Kayak*
UNDER THE MIGRANTS: *Hudson Review*
ON THE SILENT ANNIVERSARY OF A REUNION: *Chelsea*
ON EACH JOURNEY: *Chelsea*
BEYOND YOU: *Chelsea*
THEIR WEEK: *Chelsea*
OLD FLAG: *Antaeus*
THE CURRENT: *Chelsea*
SOMETHING I'VE NOT DONE: *Poetry*
TOOL: *Poetry*
BREAD: *The New Yorker*
HABITS: *Field*
A DOOR: *The New Yorker*
A DOOR: *Iowa Review*
A DOOR: *Atlantic Monthly*
A DOOR: *Sumac*
SURF-CASTING: *Iowa Review*
AT THE SAME TIME: *Poetry*
THE WHARF: *New American Review*
THE UNWRITTEN: *The New Yorker*
BEGGARS AND KINGS: *Antaeus*
SPRING: *The Nation*

THE PLACE OF BACKS: *The Nation*
DIVISION: *The New Yorker*
A PURGATORY: *Poetry*
THE CHASE: *Poetry*
A WOOD: *Choice*
NOMAD SONGS: *Choice*
THE DIGGERS: *Quarterly Review of Literature*
ANIMALS FROM MOUNTAINS: *Poetry*
SIBYL: *Iowa Review*
WHO IT IS: *Quarterly Review of Literature*
MIST: *The New Yorker*
UNDER BLACK LEAVES: *Kayak*
A SICKNESS AT THE EQUINOX: *Kayak*
WANTING A SOUL IN THE SOUTH: *Sumac*
HORSES: *The New Yorker*
SHIP: *Seneca Review*
WORDS: *Seneca Review*
ONE TIME: *The New Yorker*
THE WAY AHEAD: *The New Yorker*
SUMMITS: *Hudson Review*
TO THE HAND: *The New Yorker*
FOLK ART: *Dakotah Territory*
THE SECOND TIME: *Poetry*
EXERCISE: *Poetry*
INSTRUCTIONS TO FOUR WALLS: *The New Yorker*
WHEN THE HORIZON IS GONE: *The Berkshire Review*
THE LANTERN: *The New Yorker*
A NUMBER: *The American Scholar*
DOGS: *Hudson Review*
THE CRY: *The New Yorker*
BY THE CLOUD PATH: *Extensions*
FOREWORD: *The New Yorker*
THE PALACE: *The American Scholar*
BALLADE OF SAYINGS: *The New Yorker*
FLIES: *The Columbia Forum*

I wish to thank the Rockefeller Foundation for a grant on which I was living when this book was begun. W.S.M.

Library of Congress catalog card number 72–92616
ISBN 0-689-10556-8
Published simultaneously in Canada by McClelland and Stewart Ltd
Manufactured by Kingsport Press, Inc., Kingsport, Tennessee
Designed by Harry Ford
First Printing January 1973
Second Printing January 1974
Third Printing June 1976
Fourth Printing September 1980

FOR MOIRA

CONTENTS

Contents

WRITINGS TO AN
UNFINISHED ACCOMPANIMENT

EARLY ONE SUMMER

Years from now
someone will come upon a layer of birds
and not know what he is listening for

these are days
when the beetles hurry through dry grass
hiding pieces of light they have stolen

EYES OF SUMMER

All the stones have been us
and will be again
as the sun touches them you can feel
sun
and remember waking with no face
knowing that it was summer
still
when the witnesses
day after day are blinded
so that they will forget nothing

END OF SUMMER

High above us a chain of white buckets
full of old light going home

now even the things that we do
reach us after long journeys
and we have changed

THE DISTANCES

When you think of the distances
you recall
that we are immortal

you think of them setting out from us
all of them setting out
from us
and none dies and none is forgotten

and all over the world there are dams
lying on their backs
thinking of the sea

LOOKING BACK

Oh we have moved forward in pain

what has broken off every rock

have they each suffered
each time
wanting to stay
have they not

Before the first cell
the sands

SONG OF MAN CHIPPING AN ARROWHEAD

Little children you will all go
but the one you are hiding
will fly

THE SILENCE BEFORE HARVEST

The harps the harps
standing in fields
standing

and dark hands
playing

somewhere else the sound
sound
will arrive
light from a star

CAT GHOSTS

I

Years after
in a kitchen of another country
you're still hungry

II

In the heat of the day
your shadow comes back
to lie on your stone

LETTER TO THE HEART

Again the cry that it's late
and the islands
are just beginning to rise

MEMORY OF THE LOSS OF WINGS

An hour comes
to close a door behind me
the whole of night opens before me

THE OLD BOAST

Listen natives of a dry place
from the harpist's fingers
rain

THE DAY

If you could take the day by the hand
even now and say Come Father
calling it by your own name
it might rise in its blindness with all
its knuckles and curtains
and open the eyes it was born with

THE CLEAR SKIES

The clouds that touch us out of clear skies

they are eyes that we lost
long ago on the mountain
and lose
every day on the dark mountain
under clear skies

and because we lose them we say they are old
because they are blind we say
that they cannot find us
that their cloudy gaze
cannot touch us
on our mountain

because we have lost whoever
they are calling
we say that they are not calling
us

TO BE SUNG WHILE STILL LOOKING

Have you seen my memory
in better light
no sound for the moment
as there might
with those faces
and the gates about to close
that never do

Have you seen my memory
that hardly knew
what to do with the flags
at an age where nothing dies
but the windows are open
and same eyes
as it rolls with no echo
on the thankless roads

Have you seen my memory
after years
by fallen schools
with the smell of coats on it
and smaller coats
when there is time enough
have you seen the promises
or the tracks have you noticed
the age of the air
once it's clear

Have you seen my memory
minus the fancy words
have you looked in the cases
where I kept my mind

to tell me things
such as she lay in shallow water
in shallow water she lies
and she comes out to me
the first day
not far from home

Have you seen
my memory
the flame far from the candles

UNDER THE MIGRANTS

Winter is almost upon us
and in the south there is a battle

every day silent thunder from there
light going up like a shout

each of us is alone
when we close our eyes
the roads are strips of death

when we open our eyes the bandages
go on unwinding
back into the north the whiteness

on the avenues trucks rumble southward
to be seen no more

can you hear yourself we cannot

flocks of single hands are all flying
southward

from us

and the clocks all night all day
point that way

ON THE SILENT ANNIVERSARY
OF A REUNION

Each of these hours has been to you first
and stared
and forgotten
but I know the burnt smell
in their clothes their clothes
and know that you have at last unwoven the charred wick
into a cold black fan
and are sitting by its light
with your hands turning to stone

ON EACH JOURNEY

As on each journey there is
a silence that goes with it
to its end let us go
with each other
though the sun with its choirs of distance
rises between us though it
were to hang there the past like a day
that would burn unmoved forever
and only we went on
each alone each with nothing
but a silence

BEYOND YOU

Even when the dry wells of black honey
overflow into the winter starlight
and their stars know them at last
and taste and are young
when the shrivelled boats that have carried the sun
wake one by one face down by the river
and rise blind to sing where they are
if I can stand I will be standing by the last one
calling you
who are so near that I cannot believe you
and when I call the calling begins
beyond you

THEIR WEEK

The loneliness of Sundays grows
tall there as the light
and from it they weave
bells of different sizes
to hang in empty cupboards and in doorways
and from branches
like blossoms like fruit
and in barns
and in each room like lamps
like the light

they believe it was on a Sunday
that the animals were divided
so that the flood could happen
and on a Sunday that we were severed
from the animals
with a wound that never heals
but is still the gate where the nameless
cries out

they believe that everything
that is divided
was divided on a Sunday
and they weave the bells
whose echoes
are all the days in the week

OLD FLAG

When I want to tell of the laughing throne
and of how all the straw in the world
records the sounds of dancing
the man called Old Flag is there
in the doorway
and my words might be his dogs

when I want to speak of the sweet light
on a grassy shore
he is there
and my words have never forgotten the bitter
taste of his hands
the smell of grief in the hollow sleeves
the sadness
his shoes

and they run to him laughing
as though he had been away
they dance at his feet as though
before a throne

THE CURRENT

For a long time some of us
lie in the marshes like dark coats
forgetting that we are water

dust gathers all day on our closed lids
weeds grow up through us

but the eels keep trying to tell us
writing over and over in our mud
our heavenly names

and through us a thin cold current
never sleeps

its glassy feet move on until they find stones

then cloud fish call to it again
your heart is safe with us

bright fish flock to it again touch it
with their mouths say yes
have vanished

yes and black flukes wave to it
from the Lethe of the whales

SOMETHING I'VE NOT DONE

Something I've not done
is following me
I haven't done it again and again
so it has many footsteps
like a drumstick that's grown old and never been used

In late afternoon I hear it come closer
at times it climbs out of a sea
onto my shoulders
and I shrug it off
losing one more chance

Every morning
it's drunk up part of my breath for the day
and knows which way
I'm going
and already it's not done there

But once more I say I'll lay hands on it
tomorrow
and add its footsteps to my heart
and its story to my regrets
and its silence to my compass

TOOL

If it's invented it will be used

maybe not for some time

then all at once
a hammer rises from under a lid
and shakes off its cold family

its one truth is stirring in its head
order order saying

and a surprised nail leaps
into darkness
that a moment before had been nothing

waiting
for the law

BREAD

for Wendell Berry

Each face in the street is a slice of bread
wandering on
searching

somewhere in the light the true hunger
appears to be passing them by
they clutch

have they forgotten the pale caves
they dreamed of hiding in
their own caves
full of the waiting of their footprints
hung with the hollow marks of their groping
full of their sleep and their hiding

have they forgotten the ragged tunnels
they dreamed of following in out of the light
to hear step after step
the heart of bread
to be sustained by its dark breath
and emerge

to find themselves alone
before a wheat field
raising its radiance to the moon

27

HABITS

Even in the middle of the night
they go on handing me around
but it's dark and they drop more of me
and for longer

then they hang onto my memory
thinking it's theirs

even when I'm asleep they take
one or two of my eyes for their sockets
and they look around believing
that the place is home

when I wake and can feel the black lungs
flying deeper into the century
carrying me
even then they borrow
most of my tongues to tell me
that they're me
and they lend me most of my ears to hear them

A DOOR

You walk on

carrying on your shoulders
a glass door
to some house that's not been found

there's no handle

you can't insure it
can't put it down

and you pray please let me not
fall please please let
me not drop
it

because you'd drown like water
in the pieces

so you walk on with your hands frozen
to your glass wings
in the wind
while down the door in time with your feet
skies are marching
like water down the inside of a bell

those skies are looking for you
they've left everything
they want you to remember them

they want to write some last phrase
on you
you

A Door

but they keep washing off
they need your ears
you can't hear them

they need your eyes
but you can't look up
now

they need your feet oh
they need your feet
to go on

they send out their dark birds for you
each one the last
like shadows of doors calling calling
sailing
the other way

so it sounds like good-bye

A DOOR

Do you remember how I beat on the door
kicked the door
as though I or the door were a bad thing
later it opened
I went in
nothing
starlight
snowing

an empty throne
snow swirling on the floor
around the feet

and on an instrument
we had been trying
to speak to each other
on which we had been trying to speak
to each other for long
for time
pieces lying apart there
giving off
echoes of words our last words *implor*
    ing
    implor
    ing
by deaf starlight for a moment

and you know we
have danced in such a room
I came in late and you
were far from the door
and I had to dance with
not you after not you before

A Door

I could reach you
but this was later than anyone
could have thought

thin
snow falling
in an empty bell
lighting that chair

could I turn at all

now should I kneel

and no door anywhere

A DOOR

This is a place where a door might be
here where I am standing
in the light outside all the walls

there would be a shadow here
all day long
and a door into it
where now there is me

and somebody would come and knock
on this air
long after I have gone
and there in front of me a life
would open

A DOOR

What is dying all over the world
is a door

you will say That
is a dead thing

and you will be talking about the entry
to a chamber of your heart

you will say of that door
It is a thing

and you will be speaking of your heart

the streets will run over the wells
the wires will cover the sky
the lines will cross out the eyes
singing numbers numbers
numbers
numbers of
shadows of generations of armies with flags
the streets will run over the ears
trucks will run over the streets
no crying will be heard
nor any calling
the function of laughing neither remembered
so a tick coming over us
for no cause we by then
recognize
meanwhile in each cell the noise
turning higher as it
turns higher as it approaches

and still someone touching
a silence
an opening
may hear all around us the endless home

SURF-CASTING

It has to be the end of the day
the hour of one star
the beach has to be a naked slab

and you have to have practised a long time
with the last moments of fish
sending them to look for the middle of the sea
until your fingers
can play back whole voyages

then you send out one
of your toes for bait
hoping it's the right evening

you have ten chances

the moon rises from the surf
your hands listen
if only the great Foot is running

if only it will strike
and you can bring it to shore

in two strides it will take you
to the emperor's palace
stamp stamp the gates will open
he will present you with half of his kingdom
and his only daughter

and the next night you will come back
to fish for the Hand

AT THE SAME TIME

While we talk
thousands of languages are listening
saying nothing

while we close a door
flocks of birds are flying through winters
of endless light

while we sign our names
more of us
lets go

and will never answer

THE WHARF

for Richard Howard

From dates we can never count
our graves
cast off
our black boats our deep
hulls put out
without us

again and again we run
down onto the wharf named
for us
bringing both hands both eyes
our tongues our
breath
and the harbor is empty

but our gravestones are blowing
like clouds backward
through time to find us
they sail over us through us
back to lives that waited
for us

and we never knew

BEGGARS AND KINGS

In the evening
all the hours that weren't used
are emptied out
and the beggars are waiting to gather them up
to open them
to find the sun in each one
and teach it its beggar's name
and sing to it *It is well*
through the night

but each of us
has his own kingdom of pains
and has not yet found them all
and is sailing in search of them day and night
infallible undisputed unresting
filled with a dumb use
and its time
like a finger in a world without hands

THE UNWRITTEN

Inside this pencil
crouch words that have never been written
never been spoken
never been taught

they're hiding

they're awake in there
dark in the dark
hearing us
but they won't come out
not for love not for time not for fire

even when the dark has worn away
they'll still be there
hiding in the air
multitudes in days to come may walk through them
breathe them
be none the wiser

what script can it be
that they won't unroll
in what language
would I recognize it
would I be able to follow it
to make out the real names
of everything

maybe there aren't
many
it could be that there's only one word
and it's all we need
it's here in this pencil

every pencil in the world
is like this

SPRING

The glass stems of the clouds are breaking
the gray flowers are caught up
and carried in silence to their invisible mountain
a hair of music is flying
over the line of cold lakes
from which our eyes were made
everything in the world has been lost and lost
but soon we will find it again
and understand what it told us when we loved it

THE PLACE OF BACKS

When what has helped us has helped us enough
it moves off and sits down
not looking our way

after that every time we call it
it takes away one of the answers it had given us

it sits laughing among its friends with wrong names
all of them nodding yes

if we stay there
they make fun of us
as we grow smaller because of the melting of our bones

DIVISION

People are divided
because the finger god
named One
was lonely
so he made for himself a brother like him

named Other One

then they were both lonely

so each made for himself four others
all twins

then they were afraid
that they would lose each other
and be lonely

so they made for themselves two hands
to hold them together

but the hands drifted apart

so they made for the hands two arms

they said Between two arms
there is always a heart

and the heart will be for us all

but the heart between them
beat two ways
already for whoever

was to come

for whoever would
come after

one by one

A PURGATORY

Once more the hills
are made of remembered darkness torn off
and the eye rises from its grave
upon its old
upon its ancient life

but at a wrong moment

once more the eye
reveals the empty river
feathers on all the paths
the despairing fields
the house in which every word
faces a wall

and once more it climbs
trying to cast again
the light in which that landscape
was a prospect of heaven

everywhere
the vision has just passed out of sight
like the shadows sinking
into the waking stones
each shadow with a dream in its arms
each shadow with the same
dream in its arms

and the eye must burn again and again
through each of its lost moments
until it sees

THE CHASE

On the first day of Ruin
a crack appears running

then what do they know to do
they shout Thief Thief
and run after

like cracks converging across a wall

they strike at it
they pick it up by tails
they throw pieces into the air
where the pieces join hands
join feet run on

through the first day

while the wren sings and sings

A WOOD

for Mark and Jill Sainsbury

I have stood among ghosts of those who will never be
because of me
the oaks were darkening
we all knew who was there
sailing walking sitting as stones
ancestors ancestors I turned to say
always was it this way
from you did my shoulders learn
not to fly
my hands not to walk
my bones not to stay
from your blackbirds again and again
did I learn at evening
not to call myself home

If I don't go there
nobody's there

———

Every word
runs the hills at night

———

Smoke
remember who let you go

———

Ho it's spring
see
the echoes flying

———

Birch tree with one arm
groping in death
hold onto it

———

My cradle
was a shoe

———

We leave a child
outside
as bait for the guides

THE DIGGERS

If a man with a shovel came down the road

if two men
with shovels came down the road
if eight men with shovels
came down the road

if seventeen men with shovels came down the road
and I wanted to hide
I would see then that everything here
is transparent

yes that is what I would see but I would feel myself
then like my hand in front of my eyes
like this hand just as it is
in front of my eyes

and I would try to take it down
before they saw through it and found me

ASH

The church in the forest
was built of wood

the faithful carved their names by the doors
same names as ours

soldiers burned it down

the next church where the first had stood
was built of wood

with charcoal floors
names were written in black by the doors
same names as ours

soldiers burned it down

we have a church where the others stood
it's made of ash
no roof no doors

nothing on earth
says it's ours

When I was small and stayed quiet
some animals came
new ones each time
and waited there near me
and all night they were eating the black

they knew me they knew me
nobody saw them
I watched how they watched me
they waited right there
nobody heard them talking laughing
laughing
Laugh they told me nobody will hear

and we went out one time
onto one mountain
all the way and nobody knew we went
we went together we sounded like chewing
the next day the mountain was gone

we went out onto two mountains
we made no noise
no more noise than smoke
nobody saw us far away
the next day those mountains were almost gone

we went out
onto my dead grandmother's mountain
there an old wind lives
that's never been away
it lives on and on there alone
but the mountain's gone
and some of us
never came back all the way

SIBYL

Your whole age sits between what you hear
and what you write

when you think you're getting younger
it's the voice coming closer
but only to you

so much of your words
is the words
once they've come out of the ground
and you've written them down
on petals
if it's spring

the same wind that tells you everything at once
unstitches your memory
you try to write faster than the thread is pulled
you write straight onto the air
if it's summer

with your empty needle

straight onto a face if there's light enough
straight onto hands
if it's autumn

WHO IT IS

On the upper slope
the moon
smokes through the woods
someone is running there
silently waving
someone's father
not my father
no and not his father the drunk
no and not his
father the one that was murdered
no it is the first one
I don't know
it is his father
it is everyone I don't know
it is his father

why
is he running there

why is he running on the mountain

why is he waving why do I
not hear him
why do I not know him
why do I not know him why are they there

everywhere they have seen
their moon rising

MIST

Today seventy tongues
are hiding in the trees

their voices are hanging beyond the mist
seventy long banners mingling
red yellow
blue voices
hanging silent

here the nuthatch blows his horn
leading a thin procession of white wind

past the black trees
through the world

UNDER BLACK LEAVES

In one window
old moon swollen with our shadow
bringing it
to birth one more time

in another window
one of the stars that does not know it is the south
the birds' way

the mouse is no longer afraid of me
the moth that was clinging to my face
a day in some city
has been taken away
very old it clung there forgetting everything
nails have been drawn out of my ears

certain stars leaving their doorways
hoped to become crickets
those soon to fall even threw
dice for the months
remembering some promise

that game was long before men
but the sounds travelled slowly
only now a few
arrive in the black trees
on the first night of autumn

A SICKNESS AT THE EQUINOX

September yellows
a few of the wild laurels
from wet ditches still the loosestrife
as when I was born
and the days before

I sit in late sunlight hoping to be healed
shadows of leaves slip along me
crossing my face my chest
toward the east

to each of them
in turn I say Take
it with you

take with you leaf shape
little shadow
darkness of one leaf
where you are going
a brother or sister
you were afraid was lost for good

a mother a father
a lover
a child
from under there

WANTING A SOUL IN THE SOUTH

The world is made of less and less
to walk out on farther
and farther
another year
is about to be taken away everywhere
someone still standing there
holding a basket

the planets glide doubting
among the bare rafters here
signalling
apparently
wrong wrong this house
moving out their year
all night the cocks crow
no

it's alright though
so far
walking on in the dark
over the breathing floors
through the rooms that are here
with my basket

HORSES

The silence of a place where there were once horses
is a mountain

and I have seen by lightning that every mountain
once fell from the air
ringing
like the chime of an iron shoe

high on the cloudy slope
riders who long ago abandoned sadness
leaving its rotting fences and its grapes to fall
have entered the pass
and are gazing into the next valley

I do not see them cross over

I see that I will be lying
in the lightning on an alp of death
and out of my eyes horsemen will be riding

SHIP

Far from here but still in sight

there is a fine white ship of everything we have loved
under full sail entering
among wrecks and many bridges
where birds are watching
always watching

same
birds with one wing

forgetters of singing

here it is they see coming to them again
from those who hate them

WORDS

When the pain of the world finds words
they sound like joy
and often we follow them
with our feet of earth
and learn them by heart
but when the joy of the world finds words
they are painful
and often we turn away
with our hands of water

ONE TIME

O venerable plank burning
and your pegs with you
the hordes of flame gaining
in the marks of the adze
each mark seven times older than I am
each furthermore shaped like a tongue
you that contain
of several lives now only a dust
inside the surfaces that were once cuts
but no memory no tree
even your sparks dust
toward the last some of your old pitch
boils up through you
many children running
into a shining forest

THE WAY AHEAD

A winter is to come
　　when smaller creatures
　　will hibernate inside the bones
　　of larger creatures
　　and we will be the largest of all
　　and the smallest

A Monday is to come
　　when some who had not known
　　what hands were for
　　will be lifted and shaken
　　and broken and stroked and blessed
　　and made

An eye is to come
　　to what was never seen
　　the beginning opening
　　and beholding the end
　　falling into it

A voice is to come
　　that all the leaves
　　wanted
　　and the ears uncurled
　　to reach for
　　and one of them will hear it

Feet are already marching there
fields of green corn and black corn are already
throwing up their hands
all the weeds know and leap up from the ditches
every egg presses on toward those ends
for this the clouds sleep with the mountains

for this in the almanacs of the unborn
terrible flowers appear
one after the other
giving new light

A light is to come

SUMMITS

Mountains bloom in spring they shine in summer
they burn in autumn
but they belong to winter
every day we travel farther and at evening
we come to the same country
mountains are waiting but is it for us
all day the night was shining through them
and many of the birds were theirs

TO THE HAND

What the eye sees is a dream of sight
what it wakes to
is a dream of sight

and in the dream
for every real lock
there is only one real key
and it's in some other dream
now invisible

it's the key to the one real door
it opens the water and the sky both at once
it's already in the downward river
with my hand on it
my real hand

and I am saying to the hand
turn

open the river

FOLK ART

Sunday the fighting-cock
loses an eye
a red hand-print is plastered to its face
with a hole in it
and it sees what the palms see from the cross
one palm

THE SECOND TIME

The second time
the hills have shrunk
the bells are thinner
the hours have fewer colors
it seems that some of the old weather
must have been invented

the second time has white stone gate posts
at the head of a silent pass
under a pillar of sunlight
we see them only once
we see them only the second time
then we forget them

the second time has birds of its own
it has wings of its own
the second time comes with a picture

the second time comes with an old picture
of something not there
it clings to the picture
as to its life

death
begins the second time
with survival

EXERCISE

First forget what time it is
for an hour
do it regularly every day

then forget what day of the week it is
do this regularly for a week
then forget what country you are in
and practise doing it in company
for a week
then do them together
for a week
with as few breaks as possible

follow these by forgetting how to add
or to subtract
it makes no difference
you can change them around
after a week
both will help you later
to forget how to count

forget how to count
starting with your own age
starting with how to count backward
starting with even numbers
starting with Roman numerals
starting with fractions of Roman numerals
starting with the old calendar
going on to the old alphabet
going on to the alphabet
until everything is continuous again

Exercise

go on to forgetting elements
starting with water
proceeding to earth
rising in fire

forget fire

INSTRUCTIONS TO FOUR WALLS

Now one of you turn this way
just as you are
woman and girl all these years
speaking another language
as the earth does
and open your eyes
with the wall inside them
doubled
but going away
getting smaller and smaller
but don't you move
see how long it takes for me to appear there
and how old I am then
and how old I've been
if you can tell
but don't put on anything special for me
I want to see you as you are every day
as you see me
without my name

the one of you whose turn it is
to follow me like a dog
don't be the dog who's stolen something
don't be the dead dog
don't be the lost dog the sick dog
the watch dog
be the good brown dog that ran through both families
till you found me
be happy to see the back of my head
just where it is

and one of you be the sea
starting right there

older than words or water
opening into itself forward and backward
each wave lying still
with a piece of horizon in its arms
one sail going
one sail coming
two wings approaching each other

and one of you
stay still just as you are
with your door
be yesterday
be tomorrow
be today

IN THE LIFE OF DUST

Dust thrown into eyes
learns to see
and it follows

the first thing it sees
is a man holding dust in his hand
the next thing it sees is a hand scraping dust from the ground
the next thing it sees is the ground
and it rejoices

the next thing it sees
is footprints handprints in the ground
handprints long hollows
valleys in the earth
from scraping up dust

footprints running

the dust still feels them
remembers them coming
running
and now the dust can see

and it follows them
in its time it is everywhere
it is the dust in front of them
somewhere else waiting
watching

two men come running over the mountain
both of them blind

it sees that they are its children

and it beholds hatred
it beholds fear

A FLEA'S CARRYING WORDS

A flea is carrying a bag of diseases
and he says as he goes
these I did not make myself
we don't all have the same gifts
beginning isn't everything
I don't even know who made them
I don't know who'll use them
I don't use them myself
I just do what's in front of me
as I'm supposed to
I carry them
nobody likes me
nobody wants to change places with me
but I don't mind
I get away
bag and all
something needs me
everything needs me
I need myself
and the fire is my father

WHEN THE HORIZON IS GONE

When the horizon is gone
the body remains horizontal
the earth remains horizontal
but everything else
is vertical

the soles of the feet are vertical
so they can't climb
and they wait

the veins are vertical
so the blood can't flow
so it sinks
and there's no center to sink toward

what the hands hold is vertical
so they can't feel it
and they let go

what the eyes see is vertical
and always was
and they still don't recognize it

the sound is vertical
so they don't hear
anything

at first

calling

THE LANTERN

A little way ahead
each is alone

when you see it you are there already
in one respect

for in that world nothing can break
so no one believes in the plural there
which is the first abstraction and the last
which is the and which is the between which is the among
so no one believes in us there
so at last there is only
the single
one
alone
held together by nothing
so the question of belief never arises

that is the place of a god
for a god is alone
he sits on each different leaf
he holds in each eye
differently
in each hand differently
one emblem of one aspect of his difference
each time it is single
each time it is an image of him
each time it is an image of you
each time it is an image of no one
carrying a lantern
each time it is different
from a different side
each time it is the same

77

well once you are there can you speak

if you were going to speak at last
which would you speak to

you open your one mouth
each image opens his mouth

you say nothing
once

you open a cave in the ground
one cave
each god closes each eye
you go down inside each eye
into each vein
into each vein of each leaf
into each root
no root has an eye
it has always been so dark there

but your eye is closed
so it's lighter for you

far away an empty lantern is swinging

image of no one carrying it

you start to follow it
to see his face

APPARITION

The more like a man it is
the more it frightens the birds
the more it frightens children
the more it frightens men

it comes wanting to live
but to live

it would have to fly up in itself
it would have to clap its hands when it could say nothing
it would have to tremble at itself

A NUMBER

Those who come back from a number
are paler
they know that they're
one number the less
and whenever they talk
they talk about where they were
for each of their words has been there

and all the time they were gone
that number was here
not a day passed
without its turning up somewhere
well where then were those

who went out over unlit hills
bearing their words
to that number
and turned pale at what they saw
and keep talking about it

DOGS

Many times loneliness
is someone else
an absence
then when loneliness is no longer
someone else many times
it is someone else's dog
that you're keeping
then when the dog disappears
and the dog's absence
you are alone at last
and loneliness many times
is yourself
that absence
but at last it may be
that you are your own dog
hungry on the way
the one sound climbing a mountain
higher than time

THE WAR

There are statues moving into a war
as we move into a dream
we will never remember

they lived before us
but in the dream we may die

and each carrying
one wing as in life
we may go down all the steps of the heart
into swamp water
and draw our hands down after us
out of the names

and we may lose one by one our features
the stone may say good-bye to us
we may say good-bye to the stone
forever
and embark
like a left foot alone in the air
and hear at last voices like small bells
and be drawn ashore

and wake with the war going on

THE WATER OF THE SUNS

In craters in the west other suns went down
and by morning no one believed it
no one has to believe it the mountains
aren't selling anything
some of the suns left gold
many left water for the next time

when you spend that gold you feel the night coming on
and nothing to make a fire
under all the empty mountains

but when you drink that water you begin to wait
you hear your time falling into you out of a stone
you begin to grope through your cold veins calling
like a bird before sunrise

till the morning that needs you

A PRAYER OF THE EYES

There are stones here
that have to have been seen first
by a man many centuries old
who has gone into seven other worlds
and has come back without sleeping to look at these few stones
before going on

then the stones become visible to us as stones
but which ones are they
they are not marked in any way
those old men would not have
marked them in any way
those solitary men
why would they have wanted to mark them
after seven worlds
what mark would they have put
meaning what
on stones
that are never lost
and never anyone's

those men arrive
some of them in this lifetime
some of them only in this lifetime
sometimes somebody
sees them
may I see one of them
with his worlds behind him like wings
may I see the stones
as he sees them
may he show me the stones

THE CRY

In many houses the cry has a window
and in one house the window is open

and the cry has flowed out like one drop of water
that once filled the whole room

there it is the first drop of water
from which everything came
when it is all over

a single drop of water is flowing
there on the white path into the hills

you would see it was a tear
because it is flowing upward
becoming a note in the still night

leaving its salt to the white path
that flows into the place far below
that once was sea

as you would know
if you were to stand in that doorway
if you were to open the door
if you were to find it

of the cry
that no longer sleeps there

so that if you were to see that window
from the outside
you would see nothing

BY THE CLOUD PATH

No day has an age of its own
an entire year has no age of its own
    but there is a cloud in every picture

Those clouds are from almanacs not from calendars
    old almanacs
    taken from lovers given to prisoners
    given back
    found by children
    missing pages signed Cloud
    art is long
    a cloud is a monument to an eye

Know of the new buildings
    that some cannot be reflected in water
    all you will see reflected is clouds

    Who use those buildings sank long ago
    the question is can you still believe them

    their windows were calendars
    their moon was drawn in red
    but its heart was not there

The clouds dragging anchors are pilgrims
    the anchors are inside three sleeps
    in the prisoners
    in the lovers
    and in the children

From a window photographs of one face
    every day of its life
    are reflected rapidly on a cloud

the sound is a recording of one tone
that face produced that day
of its own

A HOLLOW

Here then is where the wolf of summer lay
heard flocks of sheep running by
like rats' teeth on the paths
heard them in the stubble like rain
listened to them pissing from their thin bones
learned one by one the tone of each jaw
grinding its dry stalks knew every cough
and by the cough the throat

here lay with the roots around him
like veins around a heart
and was the wolf of summer
there were leaves that listened to him with their whole lives
and never felt the wind
while he lay there like darkness in an ear
and hearing notes of wells
knew where the moon was

FOR SAYING THAT IT WON'T MATTER

Bones of today I am going to leave you
where you never wanted to be
listen shall we talk of it now
I am going to leave you there
every bone that is left to itself
has been in trouble
it was born to go through it
every skin is born knowing that
and each eye

you are voyaging now through the half light of my life
let us talk of this while the wind is kind
and the foam rustling on your bows
hear me I am going to leave you
on the empty shore
the sand will be blown away
we should talk about it
you were born for trouble
it is not for you that I am afraid
you will start singing camel songs

what can I say to you listen it is not for you
it won't matter to you
listen whatever you dream from then on
will be yours even if it was mine
unless it's me
listen you will still tell the fortunes of others
you will hang in the bell of earth at a wedding
you will fly on and on in white skins
by your own light

FOREWORD

We will tell no more than a little
about the first wing
the orphan

we will say nothing of his parents the giants
nor of the tree in which he was born
one autumn
nor of his sisters the grass
nor his brothers the fires

he was alone he was the first wing
it is all we need to know
everything here has two wings
except us

all we will tell
is how he found the other wing
his reflection groping downward through the air
and of the stream between them
where it rises
how flight began
why the moths
come and bathe in the dust
and it is a light to them

FINDING A TEACHER

In the woods I came on an old friend fishing
and I asked him a question
and he said Wait

fish were rising in the deep stream
but his line was not stirring
but I waited
it was a question about the sun

about my two eyes
my ears my mouth
my heart the earth with its four seasons
my feet where I was standing
where I was going

it slipped through my hands
as though it were water
into the river
it flowed under the trees
it sank under hulls far away
and was gone without me
then where I stood night fell

I no longer knew what to ask
I could tell that his line had no hook
I understood that I was to stay and eat with him

THE PALACE

for Harry Ford

Music does not happen in a place
in it leaves do not grow
even if you try to put them there
there is nothing to see and nobody knows you
even if you were born there

yet the blood continues to follow music
the heart never sleeps urging the feet of the blood
to echo to rest nowhere
to pass near the skin to listen
whether music is anywhere
to look through a glass to go on
to go through
music never waits the heart says

the blood says nothing
the deaf queen pacing alone
through her thin palace
feeling music turning in the walls

BALLADE OF SAYINGS

In spring if there are dogs they will bark
the sieves of the poor grow coarser
even in the dark we wake upward
each flower opens knowing the garden
water feels for water
the law has no face
nowhere are the martyrs more beautiful
the air is clear as though we should live forever

in summer if there are fleas there will be rejoicing
you kill the front of him I'll kill the back
every sieve knows a dance
each soldier is given a little bleached flag
ours are the only parents
the poor do not exist they are just the poor
the poor dream that their flowers are smaller
patience has the stones for a garden
the seer is buried at last in a gooseyard
the air is clear as though we should live forever

in autumn if there are trees eyes will open
one moment of freedom partakes of it all
those who will imitate will betray
the dogs are happy leading the archers
the hunter is hunted the dealer is dealt the listener is heard
the halls of government are the exhibition palaces of fear
anguish rusts
the poor believe that all is possible for others
each fruit hopes to give light
the air is clear as though we should live forever

in winter if there are feet bells will ring
snow falls in the bread of some and in the mouths of others
nobody listens to apologies
when prisoners clasp their hands a door locks
the days are polished with ashes
the cold lie in white tents hoarding sunrise
the poor we have with us always
the old vine stakes smell of the sea
the air is clear as though we should live forever

Prince it is said that night is one of the sieves
there is no end to how fine we shall be
at the names of the poor the eye of the needle echoes
the air is clear as though we should live forever

TO THE RAIN

You reach me out of the age of the air
clear
falling toward me
each one new
if any of you has a name
it is unknown

but waited for you here
that long
for you to fall through it knowing nothing

hem of the garment
do not wait
until I can love all that I am to know
for maybe that will never be

touch me this time
let me love what I cannot know
as the man born blind may love color
until all that he loves
fills him with color

THE DREAMERS

In one of the dreams men tell how they woke
a man who can't read turned pages
until he came to one with his own story
it was air
and in the morning he began learning letters
starting with A is for apple
which seems wrong
he says the first letter seems wrong

a man with his eyes shut swam upward
through dark water and came to air
it was the horizon
he felt his way along it and it opened
and let the sun out so much for the sun
and in the morning he began groping for the horizon
like the hands of a clock
day and night

a man nothing but bones was singing
and one by one the notes opened
and rose in the air and were air
and he was each one
skin mouth ears feeling
feathers he keeps counting everything
aloud including himself
whatever he counts one is missing

I think I fell asleep on a doorstep
inside someone was coming
walking on white heads that were the best words I knew
and they woke at that step for the first time and were true
when I came to myself it was morning
I was at the foot of the air

in summer and I had this name
and my hand on a day of the world

SEPTEMBER

By dawn the little owls
that chattered in the red moon
have turned into magpies in the ash trees
resting between journeys
dew stays in the grass until noon
every day the mist wanders higher
to look over the old hill
and never come back
month of eyes your paths see for themselves
you have put your hand
in my hand
the green in the leaves has darkened
and begun to drift
the ivy flowers have opened
on the weasel's wall
their bees have come to them
the spiders watch with their bellies
and along all the shores
boats of the spirit are burning
without sound without smoke without flame
unseen in the sunlight
of a day under its own king

FLIES

On the day when the flies were made
death was a garden
already without walls
without apples
with nowhere to look back to
all that day the stars could be seen
black points
in the eyes of flies
and the only sound was the roar of the flies
until the sun went down

each day after that something else was made
and something else with no name
was a garden
which the flies never saw
what they saw was not there
with no end
no apples
ringed with black stars
that no one heard
and they flew in it happily all day
wearing mourning

THE WRITING ON A FALLEN LEAF

The frost will come out under the stars
the falcons will grow thin as their voices
the fox will pretend to be old
the owl will bathe at night in the snow
the tracks of the hare will be empty shadows
I will forget

SOUTH

for Ralph Hilt

To the south in the beginning of evening a dog
barks at his echo among mountains
beyond bare walnut trees tiles are still climbing old roofs
lines of women with long burdens the colors
of dried darkening blood
each line straight into mountains
colder already all north faces
turning into their shadows
beyond them sea
through day and night to the last white mountains
an end a wise man fire
other stars the left hand

SPAN

I know hands that leapt from childhood to old age
youth was never for them however they held it
everything happened to them early or late
end of morning never found them
the entire day was a long evening
in August
they played no instrument for when would they have learned
if not in childhood
everything they did displayed impetuous prudence
and smelled of sand
they and their clumsy skills were their own age
with its two seasons

MEETING

A thirst for meeting

A long line of ghosts waiting at a well
laughing
in the evening
and I am standing among them
the line runs through me
I feel it
a procession of dry clouds

let it be clear that there is no comfort in them
comfort is far away
that lay in ambush for joy
there is no fear in them they cannot hear me
there is only that thirst
the old cracked laughing

of dry leaves
shrivelled trees broken stones
walls walls
and empty hands
held forward forever

All the gold that exists was transmuted once
by men learning to change themselves
who broke it and buried it
those who found it
took it for a metal
wanted it for its own sake
to have rather than to foresee
and for them it was evil
and they declared that transmuting it was impossible
and evil

THE INITIATE

At last a juggler is led out under the stars
tears begin to roll down his cheeks

he catches them
they fly through his hands

he sees the stars swimming up
in his tears
and he feels in his hands his tears
fly trembling through the night

what is that juggler singing
later when the morning star
is dry

he is singing Not a hair
of our head do we need to take with us
into the day

not even a hand do we need
to take with us
not even an eye
do we need to take with us
into the light

THE SEARCH

When I look for you everything falls silent
a crowd seeing a ghost
it is true

yet I keep on trying to come toward you
looking for you
roads have been paved but many paths have gone
footprint by footprint
that led home to you
when roads already led nowhere

still I go on hoping
as I look for you
one heart walking in long dry grass
on a hill

around me birds vanish into the air
shadows flow into the ground

before me stones begin to go out like candles
guiding me

GLASS

One day you look at the mirror and it's open
and inside the place where the eyes were
is a long road gray as water
and on it someone is running away
a little figure in a long pale coat
and you can't move you can't call
it's too late for that
who was it you ask

then there are many of them
with their backs to you and their arms in the air
and no shadows
running away on the road gray as ice
with the leaves flying after them
and the birds in great flocks the dust
the stones the trees
all your terrors running away from you
too late
into a cloud

and you fall on your knees and try to call to them
far in the empty face

TRAVELLING

One travels
to learn how not to look back
hearing the doors fall down the stairs
and the tongues like wet feathers in a high wind

only in the present are the voices
however far they travel
and fires raising hands between echoes

out of words one travels
but there are words along the road waiting
like parents' grandparents
we have heard of but never seen

each with its column of smoke
and its horizon beyond which nothing is known
and its sun

THE TRACK

To see that an ancestor has reappeared
as the print of a paw
in a worn brick
changes what you believe you are
and where you imagine you are going
before the clay sets

and what you think might follow you

over the floors
of the oven

the empty palace
with its many wings
its lighted stairs
its deep windows
its seasons
and its white sound
still soft underfoot

and when

PERIL

Where did you suppose the moths went
when you stopped seeing them

some that you've forgotten you ever saw
or never noticed
are standing in a circle
with their eyes inward

another joins them
coming from your window

the circle grows larger like a ring of dust
spreading on a lake of dust
it is that much harder for each of the eyes to see
in the middle of the circle the glass filament
born of a spider of air
on which is hanging and turning
the world where you are sitting
forgetting them
as the number rises
like the note of the thread

that has been too high for your ears
for a long time

THE SLEEPING MOUNTAIN

Under asters the color of my shadow
the mountain stirs in its cold sleep

dream clouds are passing through it
shaped like men lying down
with the memory of lights in them

wolf puppies from the cliffs
cry all night
when even the lakes are asleep

after the Ark was abandoned on the peak
stars appeared in it
and sailed off into the night with it

all at once it is nine years
on the plains of Troy
remembering the mountain asleep

on one wing like a human

GIFT

I have to trust what was given to me
if I am to trust anything
it led the stars over the shadowless mountain
what does it not remember in its night and silence
what does it not hope knowing itself no child of time

what did it not begin what will it not end
I have to hold it up in my hands as my ribs hold up my heart
I have to let it open its wings and fly among the gifts of the
    unknown
again in the mountain I have to turn
to the morning

I must be led by what was given to me
as streams are led by it
and braiding flights of birds
the gropings of veins the learning of plants
the thankful days
breath by breath

I call to it Nameless One O Invisible
Untouchable Free
I am nameless I am divided
I am invisible I am untouchable
and empty
nomad live with me
be my eyes
my tongue and my hands
my sleep and my rising
out of chaos
come and be given

W. S. Merwin

W. S. Merwin was born in New York City in 1927 and grew up
in Union City, New Jersey, and in Scranton, Pennsylvania.
From 1949 to 1951 he worked as a tutor in France, Portugal,
and Majorca. After that, for several years he made the greater
part of his living by translating from French, Spanish, Latin
and Portuguese. Since 1954 several fellowships have been of great
assistance. In addition to poetry, he has written articles,
chiefly for *The Nation*, and radio scripts for the BBC. He has
lived in England, France, and the United States. His earlier
books of poetry are *A Mask for Janus* (1952), *The Dancing
Bears* (1954), *Green with Beasts* (1956), *The Drunk in the
Furnace* (1960), *The Moving Target* (1963), *The Lice* (1967),
The Carrier of Ladders (1970) for which he was awarded the
Pulitzer Prize, *Writings to an Unfinished Accompaniment*
(1973) and *The Compass Flower* (1977). His translations include
The Poem of the Cid (1959), *Spanish Ballads* (1960), *The Satires
of Persius* (1961), *Lazarillo de Tormes* (1962), *The Song of
Roland* (1963), *Selected Translations 1948–1968* (1968), for
which he won the P.E.N. Translation Prize for 1968, *Transparence of the World* a translation of his selection of poems by
Jean Follain (1969) and (with Clarence Brown) *Osip
Mandelstam, Selected Poems* (1974). He has also published two
books of prose, *The Miner's Pale Children* (1970) and *Houses
and Travellers* (1977). In 1974 he was awarded The Fellowship
of the Academy of American Poets.